## Date Due

| MAR 1 1 2008 | | | |
|---|---|---|---|
| APR 1 4 2009 | | | |
| MAY 2 3 2009 | | | |
| | | | |
| | | | |
| | | | |
| | | | |
| | | | |
| | | | |
| | | | |
| | | | |
| | | | |
| | | | |
| | | | |
| | | | |
| | | | |

# Look After Yourself

# Your
# Food

# Look After Yourself

# Your Food

Claire Llewellyn

※
SEA-TO-SEA
*Mankato  Collingwood  London*

This edition first published in 2008 by
Sea-to-Sea Publications
1980 Lookout Drive
North Mankato
Minnesota 56003

Copyright © Sea-to-Sea Publications 2008
Printed in China

Library of Congress Cataloging in Publication Data

Llewellyn, Claire.
  Your food / by Claire Llewellyn.
    p.cm. -- (Look after yourself)
  ISBN 978-1-59771-098-5
  1. Nutrition--Juvenile literature. 2. Food--Juvenile literature. I. Title.

QP141.L57 2007
612.3--dc22

2006051281

9 8 7 6 5 4 3 2

Published by arrangement with the Watts Publishing Group Ltd, London.

**Series editor:** Sarah Peutrill
**Art director:** Jonathan Hair
**Design:** Kirstie Billingham
**Illustrations:** James Evans
**Photographs:** Ray Moller unless otherwise acknowledged
**Picture research:** Diana Morris
**Series consultant:** Lynn Huggins-Cooper

**Acknowledgments:**
Professor N. Russell/Science Photo Library: 18cr
Sinclair Stammers/Science Photo Library: 24t

With thanks to our models: Emilia, Holly, Jerome, Lewis, Mandalena, and Wilf

# Contents

# Food, food, food!

There are so many kinds of food. How do we know what to choose?

What shall I eat?

Food is all around us. It is even sold at the swimming pool.

I ate too much!

# Good for the body

Your body needs
food to grow,
and to stay fit
and healthy.

Different foods
help us in different
ways.

These foods give us energy.

These help us grow.

These help us
stay well.

These give us energy
and warmth.

Choose
a mixture
of foods.

# All kinds of food

You need to eat lots of different foods to stay healthy, not just your favorite food.

No foods are bad for you, but sugary foods harm your teeth.

11

# A healthy start

When you wake in the morning, your body needs food and drink.

Wake up!

Toast

Orange juice

Egg

Fruit

Cereal

Croissant

Bagel

Breakfast helps you get up and go. It helps you be active.

Don't skip breakfast!

# Keeping going

By the end of the morning, you begin to feel hungry. Time for some lunch!

My tummy is rumbling!

14

The last meal of the day gives us energy until bedtime. It allows our bodies to work all night long.

Bananas are a healthy snack.

# Check the date

The date on food packages and cans tells you when to throw them away.

Unopened, these last for years!

5 years

2 years

2 years

3 years

3 years

16

Some food lasts for a month or more in a freezer.

Fresh foods don't last long.

2 days

4 days

1 day

USE BY

14 SEP

The "best-before" date tells you how long the food will last.

# Germs spoil food

Where are the germs?

Tiny things called germs are everywhere.

On the cat

and on you!

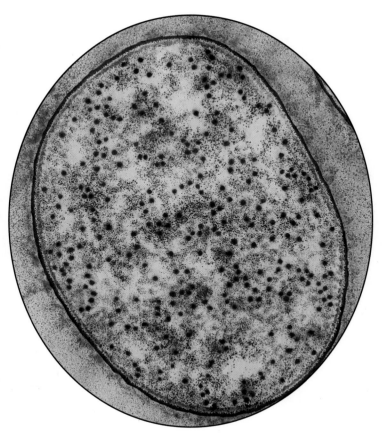

A magnified germ

18

# Germs spoil fresh food and make it go bad.

Moldy cheese

Sour milk

Bad food smells stinky!

Rotten tomatoes

# Keep food cool

Fresh foods need to be kept in the fridge. The cold helps to stop germs from spoiling them.

The fridge
will not keep
food fresh
forever.

Remember to
check the
"best-before"
date on food.

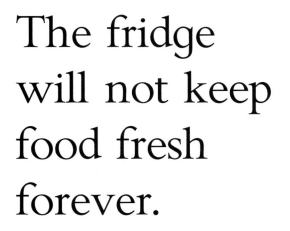

# Keep it clean

Always wash your hands with soap and water before you touch food.

Keep the kitchen clean.

Always wash fresh vegetables, fruit, and salad greens.

Remember that germs are invisible.

# Getting ready to eat

Keep food covered, or in the fridge, until you are ready to eat it.

Flies spread germs!

Cats and dogs carry germs. Don't let them touch your food.

Feed pets away from food.

25

# Eating together

It's fun to share food with family or friends.

Supper's ready!

At the end of the meal, it's time to clear up. Leave everything clean for next time.

Everything is clean.

27

# Glossary

**active**  To be moving, working, and doing things.

**best-before date**  The date on food packaging that tells you how long the food will remain safe to eat.

**energy**  The power we get from food, which lets us work, grow, and keep warm.

**fresh**  Fresh food has been made or picked recently. It is not stale, dried, canned, or frozen.

**frozen**  When something is so cold it turns hard. Frozen food can be stored for a long time.

**germs** Tiny living things that can spread disease. Germs are too small to see.

**healthy** Fit and well.

**magnified** Made to look bigger.

**moldy** Mold is a green or black fungus that can grow on food and spoil it.

**sour** Food with a sharp, nasty taste. Milk turns sour if it is left in a warm place.

**to spoil** To go bad. Spoiled food is moldy or stale and should not be eaten.

**sugar** Something that is found in many foods and makes them taste sweet.

# Index

# About this book

Learning the principles of how to keep healthy and clean is one of life's most important skills. **Look After Yourself** is a series aimed at young children who are just beginning to develop these skills. **Your Food** looks at how to have a healthy diet and teaches simple food safety rules. To encourage a positive relationship
with food it does not dwell on so-called "unhealthy" foods, but stresses a balanced diet. For older children the book could be used as a starting point to explore other food safety issues, for example, using equipment such as knives correctly and cooking food.

Here are a few suggestions for activities children could try:

**Pages 6-7** Discuss the range of places where food can be bought—supermarkets, local foodstores, outdoor markets etc.

**Pages 8-9** If appropriate, introduce the correct terms for the four food group—carbohydrates, proteins, vitamins and minerals, and fats. Children could write food diaries for a week and work out which group each food belongs to. They could then decide whether they have had a balanced diet.

**Pages 10-11** Do a class or group survey of favorite foods and present the results in a bar chart.

**Pages 12-13** Investigate what people eat for breakfast in different parts of the world by writing to pen-pals or relatives abroad.

**Pages 14-15** Discuss favorite snack foods. Which ones help children "keep going" longer?

**Pages 16-17** Collect together packaging from various different types of food and then try to find the best-before dates.

**Pages 18-19** Write "a day in the life of a germ" story. The germ may be living on a dog, then get transferred to a hand when someone strokes the dog, and so on.

**Pages 20-21** Draw stick people and decide what they might say about keeping food in the fridge.

**Pages 22-27** Make a fruit salad, following the same procedure as the two children here: keeping everything clean, washing the fruit, and keeping the food in the fridge until it's time to eat.